CASTLES ON THE RHINE

"RHEINISCHES LAND" COLLECTION

VOLUME 2

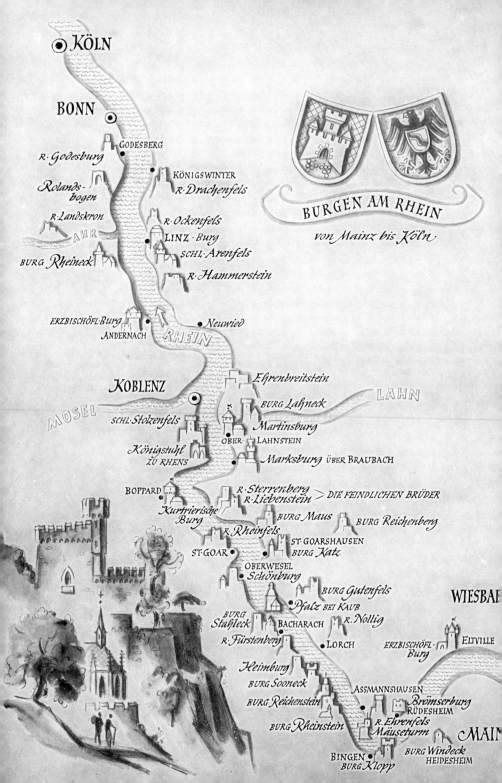

KÖLN

BONN

R. Godesburg
GODESBERG

Rolands-
bogen
KÖNIGSWINTER
R. Drachenfels

R. Landskron

R. Ockenfels
BURG Rheineck
LINZ · Burg
SCHL. Arenfels

R. Hammerstein

AHR

ERZBISCHÖFL. Burg
ANDERNACH
Neuwied

RHEIN

BURGEN AM RHEIN
von Mainz bis Köln

KOBLENZ
Ehrenbreitstein

BURG Lahneck
LAHN

MOSEL
SCHL. Stolzenfels
Martinsburg

Königstuhl
ZU RHENS
OBER-LAHNSTEIN

Marksburg ÜBER BRAUBACH

BOPPARD

R. Sterrenberg
R. Liebenstein
DIE FEINDLICHEN BRÜDER

Kurtrierische
Burg
BURG Maus
BURG Reichenberg

R. Rheinfels

ST. GOARSHAUSEN
ST. GOAR
BURG Katz

OBERWESEL
Schönburg

BURG Gutenfels
WIESBA

Pfalz BEI KAUB

BURG
Staßleck
Bacharach
R. Nollig

R. Fürstenberg
LORCH
ERZBISCHÖFL.
Burg
ELTVILLE

Heimburg
ASSMANNSHAUSEN

BURG Sooneck
Brömserburg
RÜDESHEIM

BURG Reichenstein

BURG Rheinstein
R. Ehrenfels
Mäuseturm
MAIN

BINGEN
BURG Windeck
HEIDESHEIM

BURG Klopp

CASTLES ON THE RHINE

43 Photographs with an Introduction by M. J. Mehs
New Edition Prepared by
Dr. Dr. Walther Ottendorff-Simrock

 stollfuß verlag bonn

ILLUSTRATIONS

Aero-Lloyd GmbH, Bonn: page 42; Lala Aufsberg, Sonthofen (Allgäu): pages 9, 10, 37; Fritz Ganzhübner, Mülheim: pages 22, 30; Michael Jeiter, Aachen: pages 13, 14, 18, 29, 58, 66, 70, 80, 83; Joachim Kinkelin, Worms/Rhein: page 76; Luftbild Klammet & Aberl, Germering (München): page 75; Fotoatelier Kleinz, Bingen/Rhein: page 46; Kurt Mayer, Oestrich-Winkel: page 45; Ellen Traubenkraut, Ettringen: cover picture and pages 17, 21, 25, 26, 33, 34, 38, 49, 50, 57, 61, 62, 69, 71, 72; Archiv Stadtverwaltung Koblenz: page 41; Städt. Verkehrsamt, Königswinter: page 87; Werbe- und Verkehrsamt der Stadt Bonn, Bonn - Bad Godesberg: pages 84, 88; Foto F. G. Zeitz, Königssee/Obb.: pages 53, 54, 65, 79

PICTORIAL MAP "Castles on the Rhine from Mainz to Cologne" designed by Ludwig Schäfer-Grohe, Fellbach/Stuttgart

COVER DESIGN: Gutenfels Castle

Deutsche Bibliothek Cataloguing-in-Publication Data

Castles on the Rhine / with an introd. by M. J. Mehs.
New. ed. prepared by Walther Ottendorff-Simrock.
[Engl. transl. by: Barry Jones]. - 7. ed. Bonn: Stollfuß, 1989
("Rheinisches Land" collection; Vol. 2)
Dt. Ausg. u.d.T.: Burgen am Rhein. - Franz. Ausg. u.d.T.:
Les châteaux du Rhin. - Weitere Ausg. in japan. Sprache
ISBN 3-08-615267-2
NE: Ottendorff-Simrock, Walther [Hrsg.]; GT

ISBN 3-08-615267-2

7th Edition • All rights reserved
English translation by: Barry Jones
Printed by: Becher, Brühl
89VU11

CONTENTS

INTRODUCTION

The castles on the Rhine which are such a characteristic feature of the river landscape, were created by the martial spirit of the Middle Ages as purely defensive structures, devoid of all romantic notions. They were built by powerful rulers over sacred and secular territories, on hilltops, and in the lowlands as moated castles to protect their manorial estates and their inhabitants. In most cases the work of breaking the stones and erecting the massive walls and turrets was done by feudal serfs.

Since Roman times the Rhine valley has been a line of communication of vital strategic importance. In the Middle Ages the German emperors used it for their frequent progresses into Italy and wealthy merchants sent their goods along it, up and down-stream. Obviously anyone owning a castle overlooking the valley was in a powerful position, since he was able to survey and regulate the flow of traffic across his particular territory and levy tolls on merchants. This accounts for the large number of castles along the Rhine between Mainz and Bonn, particularly in the narrow strait connecting Bingen and Koblenz. Along this stretch of the river which has a length of only 35 miles, there are more castles than in any other river valley in the world.

BOPPARD AND THE CASTLE OF THE ELECTOR BALDWIN
(Copper plate engraving by Merian, 1646)

History of the Rhine castles between Mainz and Cologne

The historical background of the Rhine castles is of such diversity that it is difficult to give a clear picture.

Ever since the time of Julius Caesar the Rhine has become more and more the real centre of the occident. The possession of a castle on the Rhine was a source of influence and power and enabled its owner to play an important part in the events of the day.

Feudal lords of every rank came to the Rhine headed by German kings and emperors in order to profit by the toll fees for which this most important waterway in the old empire offered ample opportunity. Between Mainz and Cologne there were no fewer than thirty different toll barriers. It was, therefore, only natural that every square yard of land was hotly contested and had to be tenaciously defended. This led to the construction of mighty castles which, little by little, were enlarged until they became elaborate edifices the ruins of which even today still fill us with awe. In the numerous feuds heroic resistance was often crushed by a more powerful foe and this explains the fact that in the course of time the castles frequently changed hands.

The feudal overlords

Today the Rhine between Mainz and Cologne flows through three federal states: Rhineland Palatinate, Hesse and North Rhine-Westphalia. But you need only cast a glance at an historical map showing Germany at about the time of the Peace of Westphalia (1648) to see how many independent territories and political groups vied with each other for possession of these seats of power on the Rhine in their search for influence and domination of what can truly be described as Germany's river of destiny. No great change took place in this state of affairs until the French Revolution and the Congress of Vienna.

The former Knight's Hall in the Marksburg · Text on page 64

BACHARACH AND STAHLECK CASTLE
(Copper plate engraving by Wenzel Hollar around 1638)

In the Middle Ages the Electorate of Mainz was firmly in possession of the upper Rhine because it held the castle of Elfeldt, known today as *Eltville* which, strange to say, had originally been built by the Elector Baldwin of Trier as a defence against Mainz but which he soon ceded to Mainz. But above all the castles of *Klopp* and *Ehrenfels* at the entrance to the Binger Loch, together with the *Mouse Tower* were held by the Mainz Elector. The same applied to *Rheinstein* which about the year 1350 had been in the possession of the Trier Elector for a brief period; and to the castle of *Reichenstein* which was originally a Palatine possession, and the castles of *Sooneck* and *Heimburg*. No traveller along the Rhine could possibly evade this impregnable barrier of toll fortresses many of which were occupied by robber knights.

Further downstream the Elector Palatine staked his claim to the posses-sion first of *Fürstenberg Castle*, formerly belonging to the Cologne Electors which had meanwhile been conquered by Ludwig of Bavaria for a time.

11

14th century carved gravestone of a knight in the Liebfrauenkirche at Oberwesel

Then he sought possession of *Stahleck* which had likewise first belonged to the Cologne Electors and afterwards passed into the hands of the Counts of Katzenelnbogen, various German emperors and finally to the Palatinate in 1214. Further claims by the Elector Palatinate were to the *Pfalz* near Kaub built by Ludwig of Bavaria and to *Gutenfels* built by the Falkensteiners which became Ludwig of Bavaria's favourite residence. The *Schönburg* near Oberwesel, however, property of the Counts of Schönburg, lay within the territory of the Trier electors.

Around St. Goar and St. Goarshausen the Counts of Katzenelnbogen and after their demise about 1500, the Landgrave of Hesse came from the East to dominate the scene, holding *Rheinfels* Castle on the left bank, *Katz* Castle on the right bank and the *Marksburg*. As the counterpart, so to speak, there was the *Maus* Castle near Wellmich held by the Electors of Trier who exercised territorial rights over an extensive area on both sides of the river from the mouth of the Moselle in Koblenz up to Boppard and beyond. The castle in *Boppard, Stolzenfels* Castle and *Ehrenbreitstein* are significant witnesses to the power of the Trier electorate as is also the *Kurfürstenburg* in Koblenz which belongs to the Moselle area rather than to the Rhine. In between were the legendary knights' castles of *Sterrenberg* and *Liebenstein* known as the "Enemy Brothers". The former had originally been in Palatine possession, the latter for a time having been held by Trier. And near Rhens there was an enclave belonging to the Cologne electors together with *Lahneck* and *Martinsburg* which were the most northerly toll-posts of the Mainz electorate.

Near Neuwied a new series commences: first with the County of Wied and then in *Andernach* with the Kaiserpfalz, a gift of the Emperor Barbarossa to the Cologne electorate. Downstream from here there are alternate electorates: Trier owned *Hammerstein* and *Arenfels* (which had previously belonged to the Isenburgs); Cologne *Rheineck* (once Palatinate) the castle on the *Drachenfels* and the *Godesburg* together with the Dukedoms of Jülich and Berg extending as far as Cologne which was itself a free imperial city.

Each one of these castles led a life of its own and experienced a chequered history in the service of its various owners. However, what interests us above all is the common destiny that befell them all and we cannot help asking why not a single one of them has been preserved in its original form. When and for what reasons were they destroyed or allowed to fall into decay?

12

Inner courtyard of the Pfalz near Kaub · Text on page 55

The first attack on the Rhine Castles

The 13th century saw the first major attack on a number of castles for which, however, their owners who played an inglorious part, had only themselves to blame. The election of Rudolf of Habsburg had been preceded by a deplorable interregnum, a time of internal disintegration during which the brigandage of the robber knights spread. It was in order to fight this plague that the League of Rhenish Towns had been founded in 1254 which joined forces with the spiritual electors to keep the trade routes and especially the Rhine open to traffic. But this individual initiative on the part of the towns proved to be inadequate; their warriors had, for example, made a vain attack on *Rheinfels* Castle. It was not until King Rudolf raised his powerful arm against them in 1272 that the robbers' dens on the Rhine and elsewhere were relentlessly and mercilessly destroyed. These centres of the robber knights were the castles of *Rheinstein, Reichenstein* and *Sooneck* near Bingen and *Rheineck* near Niederbreisig. The castles were destroyed and summary justice administered to the felons. The robbers' fortress of *Rheinfels* alone proved unassailable.

The Thirty Years' War

The second great onslaught on the Rhine castles came with the religious wars of the 16th and 17th centuries. First there was the turmoil in and around Cologne between 1582 and 1586 which resulted in an imperial reprimand of the Cologne Archbishop Gebhardt Truchsess von Waldburg because he had been converted to the new faith, in consequence of which the castles of *Drachenfels* and *Godesburg* were destroyed. Then the Thirty Years' War, that ill-fated struggle for power between the two confessional factions, brought tribulation to many a Rhine castle. At that time soldiers from all over Europe — imperial troops, soldiers of the Catholic "League" and the Protestant "Union", Frenchmen, Spaniards and Swedes fought for supremacy in the Rhine valley. Each of the belligerents sought to occupy and hold on to the most important strategic positions in this grave ideological struggle. *Eltville,* in those days still known as Elfeldt, *Klopp* Castle, *Ehrenfels* and *Fürstenberg* were held by the Swedes; *Stahleck, Gutenfels* and *Schönburg* were successively attacked and plundered by the Spaniards,

15

The Pfalz near Kaub and Gutenfels Castle · Text on page 55

the French and the Swedes; *Ehrenbreitstein* was captured by the French, *Koblenz* by the Swedes; *Andernach, Hammerstein, Rheineck* and *Drachenfels* were occupied and in some cases bombarded and burnt down by Swedish, imperial and Spanish troops.

The Reunion Wars

The third and for most of the castles, more destructive danger for the region of the Middle Rhine came with the decisions of the Metz Reunion Chamber under the French King Louis XIV. In order to gain sovereignty over German territories, he sent his armies as far as the Rhine to protect his own troops from the rear, conquering and destroying one castle after the other. In 1688 *Klopp, Reichenstein* and *Lahneck* fell; in 1689 *Ehrenfels, Sooneck, Heimburg, Fürstenberg, Stahleck, Schönburg, Maus, Stolzenfels, Andernach, Hammerstein* and *Rheineck*. Of all the beleaguered fortresses Rheinfels was again the only one to withstand even the French attacks.

The period of the French Revolution

The fourth and final blow to be inflicted on the Rhine castles came in the time of the French Revolution. After the canonade of Valmy in 1792 the revolutionary troops forced the German armies to withdraw beyond the Rhine. Those Rhine castles that were still standing or which had been rebuilt and were manned for resistance, were forced to capitulate. The walls were razed to the ground, the stones sold and the occupants expelled. Such was the fate especially of *Gutenfels, Katz, Maus, Rheinfels, Lahneck* and the *Godesburg*.

Since the French Revolution there has no longer been any real history of the Rhine castles. Their former significance was a thing of the past since they were no longer of any use for war purposes and offered no protection against modern artillery and explosives. A few which had not fallen entirely into decay and could be made habitable, became permanent or summer residences.

16

Nollig Castle near Lorch · Text on page 51

The Rhine landscape and the castles

The castles on the Rhine were at one time a part of history. They do not appear as foreign bodies in the landscape but seem to have merged with it and no Rhine traveller of today could imagine this landscape without them. The men who built them were both artists and landscape designers quite unlike the more technically-minded builders of today.

The ancient castles on the Rhine are the work of the creative German spirit and artistic design far beyond the mere functional edifice built for defensive purposes. In their massive ground plans they are hardly less impressive than the romanesque Gothic cathedrals on the Rhine with their spires soaring heavenwards. Where the Rhine landscape, the landscape of "Germany's pulsating artery" — as Görres once described it — called for some distinguishing feature, the builders of these castles provided it. And they did so with such assurance and vitality that they appear to have grown naturally out of the living rock. When one inspects the individual castles more closely — their gates and turrets, their courtyards and chambers, their spiral staircases and apartments, one finds at every turn that each century, each period of artistic style left behind its own typical architecture which, in some cases must even be described as unique in its beauty. Where the interior of the castles have escaped destruction, there are castle chapels, art collections, libraries, archives and arsenals containing all kinds of weapons to prove that the feudal lords of these castles led lives of culture, that they were truly representative of the centuries in which they lived, being both patriots and protectors of the landscape, creators and patrons of science and the arts who made their castles real centres of life and culture.

The castle as a structure of defence and defiance

With what idea in mind were these castles built? In accordance with what laws were they planned and further developed? The following outline is intended to answer these questions since it contains all the components of a castle fortress.

Originally castles were intended to be fortified residences for feudal lords who sought to protect themselves against attack. The earliest form of

19

The Mouse Tower in the Binger Loch

castle, therefore, was a building with very thick walls the ground floor of which, apart from having a gate that could be securely barred from the inside, revealed scarcely any other opening. The gate was particularly well protected on the outside by a deep moat which could only be crossed by a drawbridge. In the course of time additions were made to this early kind of fortress according to the space available. In most cases the first addition was a courtyard protected from the outside world, of course, by a high wall surmounted by battlements and parapets, sometimes with its own gatehouse for the operation of the drawbridge. Subsequently further outbuildings were added round the courtyard which were always protected against any potential attacker by strong walls. These outbuildings gradually assumed the functions originally concentrated in the central building.

The central building or *palas* (marked in the sketch as 1) contained the residential quarters of the lord or knight and included the kitchen, living rooms, ladies' retiring rooms, a banqueting hall, the baronial hall, sleeping quarters and other accommodation such as a library and a room for hunting trophies.

At a point giving the most favourable view of the surrounding countryside was the *keep* (2), a tall tower with pinnacles and turrets towering above the surrounding buildings. This was the look-out from which all movements and changes in the vicinity of the castle as well as beyond could be observed. During an assault on the castle it was the central command post from which the defence of the castle was directed. At times the underground vaults were used as dungeons unless some other part of the subterranean quarters was used for this purpose.

Attached to the residential quarters or forming part of them was the *Castle Chapel* (3), often a building of great architectural beauty. The castle chaplains were, in many cases, descended from the same noble family as their overlords.

Where space permitted and the need existed there were the necessary *service quarters* (4) such as servants' rooms, toll house, stables, barn, granary, tithe barn, workshop, smithy, arsenal, carpenter's shop, well-house, brewery, poultry house, peacock house — some of them located over the mighty vaulted cellars which contained a plentiful supply of mature wines stored in massive casks.

Schönburg Castle above Oberwesel · Text on page 56

DIAGRAMMATIC LAY-OUT OF A CASTLE
1 living quarters (palas), 2 Keep, 3 Chapel, 4 Service or Domestic buildings, 5 Outworks, 6 Drawbridges,
7 Turrets, 8 Defensive gallery

All that has been described so far formed part of the *Main Castle,* in front of which were the *outer works* of the castle. It is astonishing how the builders managed to utilize every fissure, protrusion and slope in the solid rock for the purpose of the castle. The *outer works* (5) were a kind of outer court for the main fortification, secured on all sides by *drawbridges* (6) and no less protected than the Main Castle by buttresses and battlements, *turrets* (7), parapets, shooting slits and machicolations, with *ramparts* (8) garrets and pinnacles. The outer works also had their own gatehouse which was specially protected by a portcullis.

The construction and completion of a castle continued, in most cases, over a period of centuries; because again and again new means of improving its defences were discovered. Every castle is thus a variation of the same theme, a highly peculiar alternation between walls, moats and battlements, between courtyards, inner and outer baileys, ramparts and outer bastions, prison yards and dungeons, residential quarters and service buildings, outer, middle and inner gates.

23

Katz Castle above St. Goarshausen · Text on page 59

Even though all these features do not apply to every castle on the Rhine, the above general description is, on the whole, accurate.

The castles in the poetry of the 18th and 19th centuries

Perched on the mountain peaks — or, as is more often the case with the Rhine castles — clinging to their slopes, the castles on the Rhine have a particular fascination for people today, even though they have faded into the background of history. This is also the way travellers felt as they sailed up and down the Rhine at the beginning of last century: Dutchmen and Englishmen, Frenchmen and Germans. And their experience of the great river was expressed in the words of the poets, one of the greatest of them being *Goethe* in his younger years, already known for his "Götz" and "Werther" who, at the sight of one of the Rhine castles was inspired to write his poem "Hoch auf dem alten Turm". In July 1774 he was

DRACHENFELS CASTLE
(Copper plate engraving by Merian, around 1640)

24

Heimburg Castle in Niederheimbach · Text on page 48

travelling down the River Lahn together with Lavater and Basedow and when the Rhine valley opened up before him and he set eyes for the first time on *Lahneck* Castle, he wrote: "Hoch auf dem alten Turme".

These verses are a milestone in the history of German poetry. The emergence of the Rhine in German literature, the awareness of the grandeur of Germany's past and all that later played such a great and lasting role in the romantic beauties and associations of the Rhine and its castles, springs from Goethe's first sight of Lahneck Castle.

Hölderlin's first impression of the Rhine which he recorded in his travel journal in 1788, Count *Friedrich Leopold von Stolberg's* description of his journey from Bonn to Mainz (1791/92) and also the magnificent account given by *Heinrich von Kleist* of his Rhine trip in 1801, mark the beginning of that flood of 19th century travel reports in which so much space is devoted to the Rhine and its castles. Typical of many writers of that time was the work of *Johanna Schopenhauer,* the philosopher's mother, who in her "Excursion to the Rhine" (1816) recorded her impressions of the castles as follows: "Imagine, in addition to the sublime splendour of natural beauty, the many picturesque ruins of old castles gazing sternly down from the rocky eminences into the valley. During the whole length of our journey we were within sight of at least one such ruin, often of more than one, and each has its distinctive peculiarities of architecture and situation. I felt that I was turning over the leaves of some old collection of landscape prints, so rapidly does one interesting scene follow on the heels of the last. In truth one has not eyes to see everything. Behind Assmannshausen the ruins of Sooneck Castle sit enthroned on a high rock; and just beyond this the river widens out until it almost resembles a lake, on which to my astonishment I thought I beheld a great warship with spreading sails; but it was the Pfalz, a castle built in the middle of the Rhine. Opposite are the dark walls of the old town of Kaub, and high above these again the proud ruins of Gutenfels Castle. Behind the pleasant little town of St. Goar rise the walls of Rheinfels which was destroyed in the Revolutionary Wars. More ruins overlook St. Goarshausen, and at an angle from this, in the distance, the remains of two further castles are visible. I cannot describe to you the beauty and sublimity of this landscape which now at sunset lay pink and glimmering before us. I could not tear myself away from it until all had faded in the last embers of the dying sun."

27

Reichenstein Castle near Trechtingshausen · Text on page 47

Symbols of Rhine romanticism

Josef von Eichendorff while still a student at Heidelberg, paid homage to the castles of the Middle Rhine in his poem "Auf einer Burg", and *Clemens* and *Bettina Brentano,* that brother and sister who had so much spiritually in common, held romantic dialogues with the ruins of the Rhine castles. The castles became the symbols of Rhine romanticism. Poets of the Wars of Liberation like *Max von Schenckendorf, Ernst Moritz Arndt* and others glorified them in their songs. Scholars like *Nikolaus Vogt* and *Karl Simrock,* after years of painstaking research as collectors and compilers, published their Rhine sagas which, in the course of the centuries had become as much an integral part of the castles as the ivy clinging to their grey walls.

An international heritage

The poets of other nations too have paid tribute to the romanticism of the Rhine castles. In the first chapter of her book "De l'Allemagne", *Madame de Staël* who sees the Rhineland landscape with the eyes of a *Friedrich Schlegel,* speaks of the "débris des châteaux forts", and *Victor Hugo,* leading figure in French romanticism, colourfully portrays the romantic world of ruined castles in his "Le Rhin" which appeared in Paris in 1841. But before this, in 1816, *Byron,* in the third canto of his "Childe Harold's Pilgrimage", had written: "The castled crag of Drachenfels/ Frowns o'er the wide and winding Rhine".

The Rhine and its castles also form the romantic background to *Longfellow's* "The Golden Legend" (1843). And so the castles on the Rhine had become part of the cultural heritage of almost the entire civilized world.

Castle-lovers to the rescue

When the Rolandsbogen, a ruined arch above Rolandseck, collapsed on New Year's Eve, 1840, *Ferdinand Freiligrath,* who was then living in Unkel, published a passionate appeal for the reconstruction of the ruin. This appeal resulted in numerous lovers of the Rhine castles making gener-

Fürstenberg Castle above Rheindiebach · Text on page 51

THE FORTIFICATION OF EHRENBREITSTEIN
AT THE TIME OF THE THIRTY YEARS' WAR
(Copper plate engraving by Merian 1646)

ous contributions which enabled the arch to be rebuilt by the Cologne Cathedral architect, *E.F. Zwirner.*

The Biedermeier style which followed the period of romanticism from about 1830 onwards and which Günter Weydt described as "a style of conservation and collecting", gave a powerful stimulus to all efforts aimed at that time at preventing the increasing decay of the castles and at ensuring their preservation for posterity. There were more or less successful attempts partially or entirely to rebuild the ruins and to fit them out as summer residences for the nobility. Their new owners then sought to fill the castles with new life, a life "characterized by the spirit of the Middle Ages". They filled the rooms with old furniture from past centuries or with artistic reproductions in the Biedermeier style. By introducing collections of paintings and coats of arms, an assortment of glassware and pewter, suits of armour, weapons, documents and books the castles acquired the character of a museum.

The Prussian royal family took a particular interest in this revival of the Rhine castles: King Friedrich Wilhelm IV commissioned the architect Friedrich Karl *Schinkel* to rebuild the ruins of *Stolzenfels* Castle, which had

31

View of Bacharach from Stahleck Castle · Text on page 52

been presented to him by the city of Koblenz, in a neo-Gothic style with a proliferation of towers and turrets. Crown-Prince Friedrich Wilhelm and Prince Friedrich of Prussia who were now the owners of the castles of *Sooneck* and *Rheinstein,* had them rebuilt in the same style. They were then furnished in such a way as to make them equally acceptable as residences or as museums. The same was done for *Rheineck* Castle near Niederbreisig. Its artistic owner Moritz August von Bethmann-Hollweg, engaged Josef Karl *Lassaulx* to redesign the castle in 1832.

Stahleck Castle above Bacharach · Text on page 52

Historicism and the care of ancient monuments

Although the love of ancient castles that prevailed in the Romanticist period and the fashion of collecting and conservation of the Biedermeier years never entirely disappeared but have continued to the present day, the historicism of the latter half of the 19th century gave greater scope to a scientific approach to the study of history. At the end of the 19th and the beginning of the 20th century views changed once again. The old castles became a subject of interest in the field of the care of ancient monuments, that is to say they "incorporated an historical and cultural value which was to be conserved and cultivated" (*Magnus Backes*). At this point tribute must be paid to the work of an association which had set itself the task of preserving the castles and of conducting scientific research into all questions connected with medieval fortifications. This was the *Association for the Preservation of German Castles* which was founded in 1899. For many years the driving force in this association was the architect *Bodo Ebhardt* who, himself, conducted much research into German castles. As custodian of the *Marksburg* he distinguished himself by his reconstruction of that castle in the historic medieval style and also by his work in restoring and protecting numerous other German castles. Bodo Ebhardt was also responsible for the creation of the largest library in Europe consisting of books devoted to medieval castles. Today the *Deutsche Burgenvereinigung zum Schutz historischer Wehrbauten, Schlösser und Wohnbauten e.V.* at Marksburg near Braubach, is continuing the work of the original association in an exemplary manner. It is the main information centre for all questions connected with castle building and restoration work. It is planned to set up a German Castles Research Institute based on the library mentioned above and including archives covering all German fortified buildings and castles, a card index system for German castles and the picture archives at present being compiled.

35

Gutenfels Castle and the Pfalz near Kaub · Text on page 55

The Present

As a result of two world wars and the continued influence of materialism, the general attitude to these ancient castles has again undergone a change. The more we turn our backs on romanticism and historicism, the more do practical considerations take priority. Insofar as the castles are thought about at all, they are looked upon from the point of view of the use to which they can be put and the advisability of investing money in them. Most of them are now open to visitors and offer facilities for refreshment. Some of them like *Rheinstein, Sooneck, Marksburg* and *Stolzenfels,* are museums; others like *Stahleck, Schönburg Katz Castle* and *Gutenfels,* are youth hostels. While their parents and grandparents were content with no more than a fleeting glance at the castles on the Rhine, the young people of today live in them and with them, gaining a new understanding of history and a respect for the achievements of former generations. For instance, when members of the youth groups belonging to the European Union meet at *Gutenfels* Castle, their discussions are inspired by a living historical consciousness which is more than a mere musty veneration. Many of them realize that the Rhine castles are not merely dead relics of a time long since past but that they have become a living part of the process of time, a time in which people see a new and meaningful purpose for these grey guardians of this great European river.

36

Klopp Castle above Bingen · Text on page 44

THE RHINE CASTLES

The Archbishop's Castle in Eltville Picture on page 38

The Episcopal Castle on the banks of the Rhine at Eltville with its defiant-looking keep is a landmark that is visible far and wide. It was built in 1332 by the factious Archbishop Balduin of Trier and Luxemburg, a minion of the Emperor Ludwig of Bavaria as "Defiant Mainz", as the Pope had raised Heinrich von Virneburg to the See of Mainz. After 1330 the Archbishop's Castle was the preferred residence of the Archbishops of Mainz for about 150 years. Archbishop Heinrich von Virneburg completed the building of the castle after Balduin's death. In 1636 it was destroyed by the Swedes operating from the "Eltviller Aue" but the castle tower has remained intact right down to the present day. The entire lay-out of the castle formed the south-east cornerstone of the town fortifications which had been constructed by Archbishop Balduin following the award of municipal rights on August 23rd 1332.

Johannes Gutenberg, the inventor of Book-printing with movable letters received here the only tribute paid to him during his lifetime. Living in poverty in Mainz the inventor whose life's work had remained unrecognized in his native city, was made a court nobleman by Duke Adolf II of Nassau on January 17th 1465. At the same time he was given an annuity for life of 240 bushels of corn and 2 vats (2000 litres) of wine which he had to consume in his house. In the tower of the electoral castle a memorial centre has been set up in memory of Gutenberg.

The castle today is the culture centre of the town of Eltville and is used by the town authorities for receptions, concerts and as a permanent gallery.

Owned by the Municipality of Eltville. Gutenberg Memorial Centre, guided tours, inspection possible throughout the year except January. Closed on Mondays. — Reache by car from the Rhine embankment; car park, from there 3 minutes walk. Information: Eltville Tourist Office.

The Archbishop's Castle in Eltville · Text on page 39

Windeck Castle in Heidesheim

This little moated castle situated at the northern end of Heidesheim, in addition to a moat formed by a diversion of the Sülzbach and the remains of the interior defensive wall, also possessed a circular wall which, today, has entirely disappeared. The best preserved part of the castle is its massive tower which is probably the oldest residential tower in Hesse, having been built by Herdegen von Winternheim about the year 1200. All that is left of the wooden parapet walk which used to circumvent the tower are a few old beams. The building housing the living quarters and located round three sides of the tower, dates from the end of the 16th century.

When the last of the Winternheim family died towards the end of the 14th century, the property passed into the possession of the Mainz Electorate which then assigned the castle to its district administrator as his official residence.

From 1609 onwards at the latest, it was an hereditary castle and had various owners, one of them being Jan van Werth, famous cavalry general of the Thirty Years' War. When the castle and its contents were auctioned by the French, Windeck Castle, formerly also known as Wintereck, passed into private ownership.

Owned by Käthe Wehner. Inhabited. — Not open to the public.

The Three Castles in Rüdesheim

The castles of the Knights of Rüdesheim today still dominate the scene in this old wine town.

The Lower Castle of *Brömserburg* was probably built as a moated castle about the year 1000 and is today still one of the most notable examples of Romanesque castle architecture. Grouped around the mighty keep, it was used until well into the 13th century by the archbishops of Mainz who, in the years that followed, handed it over to the Brömser family of Rüdesheim. Today the Brömserburg houses the *Rheingau Museum.*

Owned by the town of Rüdesheim. Rheingau Museum and Wine Museum. — Reached by car; Car park. — Open to the public from March 1st to November 15th from 9 a.m. to 12 noon and from 2 p.m. to 5 p.m. (except Mondays).

40

The German Corner · Text on page 74

The Upper Castle of Boosenburg is also a former moated castle, occupied since the 13th century by the Füchse family of Rüdesheim and between 1474 and 1830 by the Barons Boos von Waldeck. Frequent alterations were made to the castle and only the early Romanesque tower which is 38 metres high is still standing.

Owner: Dr. Carl Jung and Co., Vineyard and Wine Distillery. — Not open to the public.

The *Markthurg* situated close to the market place is one of the oldest castles in the Rheingau. It belonged to the "Herren vom Markte" (Lords of the Market), a family which died out in the 16th century. All that remains of the castle is the Romanesque tower some 25 metres high.

Owned by Vineyard Johann Schön Erben. Inhabited. — Reached by car. — On view subject to owner's consent.

The Niederwald Monument

Picture on page 42

When in 1871 following the end of the Franco-German War, the German federal states united to form the German Reich, it was decided to set up a national monument to commemorate this important event in history. Among the many proposals put forward for the site of the monument, the Niederwald above Rüdesheim was selected — an area much extolled by the poets of the Romantic era. The foundation stone was laid on September 16th 1877. The monument was constructed in accordance with the designs of the sculptor Professor Dr. Johannes Schilling and the architect Professor Dr. Karl Weisbach. The construction work took six years at the end of which the inaugural ceremony took place in the presence of Emperor Wilhelm I on September 28th 1883.

The principal figure portrays Germania holding the imperial crown in her raised right hand and the sword of the Reich in her left hand. The monument is 37.6 metres high and cost 1,200,000 Marks, about a third of which was raised by public donations.

A footpath leads to the monument through the vineyards from Rüdesheim. Cabin cable cars run from the centre of Rüdesheim to the monument — a beautiful ride which is recommended on account of the delightful views of the Rhine valley and the surrounding countryside.

43

The Niederwald Monument · Text on page 43

Klopp Castle above Bingen

Picture on page 37

Klopp Castle, one of the rare hilltop castles on the Rhine, was built on the foundations of a Roman fortress (Roman well). In 1420 the castle passed into the possession of the Mainz Cathedral Chapter on whose orders it was demolished in 1713. In 1789, in the course of the Palatinate War of Succession, it was rebuilt. Since 1897 it has been the office of the municipal administration.

The tower of Klopp Castle houses the local history museum containing some valuable collections. Here the instruments of a Roman doctor of the 2nd century after Christ are particularly worth seeing.

Owned by the town of Bingen. Houses the local municipal administration. Local hostory museum in the Castle Tower. (Open to the public daily from Good Friday to mid-October. In the annex of Klopp Castle: café-restaurant with the Rhinegold Hall. Reached by car; car park in the immediate vicinity of the castle.

Ehrenfels Castle near Rüdesheim

Picture on page 45

The Mainz electoral castle dating from the first half of the 13th century, together with Klopp Castle on the opposite side and the Mouse Tower formed a solid defence of the electorate to the North. Situated half-way up the rock-side at the entrance to the Binger Loch, it was a vital strategic point in the Middle Ages located as it was, fairly low overlooking the river. At the same time the Ehrenfels toll was an important source of revenue for the Mainz archbishops who enlarged and improved it in accordance with its importance, making it one of the most magnificent castles on the Rhine. In times of war the treasures of Mainz Cathedral were stored there. The castle was destroyed in 1689 but with its mighty face wall facing the hill on which it stands and flanked by two circular corner towers, the ruins present a most picturesque scene. Those prepared to make the effort to climb the steep paths leading through the vineyards will be well rewarded by the beautiful view of the Rhine valley which Karl Simrock described as "one of the most glorious, even perhaps the most magnificent to be seen anywhere in the Rhine valley".

Owned by the Land of Hesse. Administration of state vineyards in Eltville. — Reached on foot in 45 minutes from Rüdesheim. — Closed to the public owing to the danger of collapse. Barbecue facilities in the former castle garden.

The ruins of Ehrenfels Castle near Rüdesheim · Text on page 44

Rheinstein Castle

Picture on page 46

Situated only 90 metres above the river, built on a projecting rock widely visible from a distance, Rheinstein Castle, formerly known as Voitsburg or Feitsburg. The castle was first mentioned in ancient documents in connection with the Ottonian gifts by Emperor Otto III to the Archbishopric of Mainz — customs stronghold — mentioned (983—1002). In the 11th and 12th centuries it was used by the Electorate and Archbishopric of Mainz as a defensive and offensive castle. The highlight of the castle's splendour was the stay of Rudolf I of Habsburg 1282—1286. He declared the castle a "Castle Law Court" and gave it the name "Königstein". From here he put an end to the activities of the robber knights and founded the "noble knighthood". From the 14th to the 17th century the castle was granted in tenure to the Archbishops of Mainz.

In 1825 the art-loving Prince Friedrich of Prussia acquired the ruins of the castle which he had rebuilt in the neo-Gothic style. Today Rheinstein Castle is furnished as a residential castle and is again open to the public. Of particular interest are the glass paintings dating from the 15th century, the furniture from the 15th and 19th centuries and the armour from the 15th century.

Owned by Herman Hecher. Open to the public daily from 9 a.m. to 7 p.m. Closed from December to February. Reached by car from Koblenz and Bingen (B9). Car park below the castle. — 5 minutes walk from the car park. — Information available in foreign languages.

Reichenstein Castle

Picture on page 26

Above St. Clement's Chapel (8th century) romantically situated on the banks of the river, and at the end of the Morgenbach Valley, rises Reichenstein Castle, one of the oldest castles on the Rhine. First mentioned in 1213 as the possession of Kornelimünster Abbey which had it administered by a castellan, this castle developed into a den of robber knights and, in 1253, it was destroyed for the first time by the League of Rhenish Cities. Then in 1282 it was Rudolf von Habsburg who had it razed to the ground — the castle having in the meantime passed into the possession of the Mainz electorate and having been rebuilt. After again being restored, the castle was, for a long time, a bone of contention between the electorates of Mainz and the Palatinate. The imposing outer wall facing the hillside probably dates from the 14th century. In 1689 it was again destroyed,

47

Rheinstein Castle above Trechtingshausen · Text on page 47

this time by the French. But it was rebuilt in 1900 by the grandfather of the present owner and today houses a very important *collection of antlers and weapons.*

Owned by Hermann Freiherr von Schorlemer. Valuable collections. Castle Hotel with restaurant. — Reached by car from Trechtingshausen via the B9; car park in the castle courtyard. — 5 minutes walk from the B9. — Open to the public with guided tours daily every 40 minutes. (Closed November and December). For large parties prior notification necessary. Telephone: Bingen 06721-6117 or 6101.

Sooneck Castle Picture on page 49

Sooneck is the frontier fortress on the edge of the Soon Forest, the fringe of which extends almost down to the Rhine valley. It is one of the oldest castles on the Rhine. The original building was constructed in the 11th century for the protection of the Kornelimünster Monastery. In the 13th century it was already notorious as a den of robber knights. It is one of the castles that were besieged and destroyed by King Rudolf von Habsburg in order to bring peace to the area. In about 1350 it was again rebuilt. In 1689 the castle was in ruins, and it was acquired by Crown Prince Friedrich Wilhelm of Prussia in 1834 from the town of Niederheimbach. He had it rebuilt in the neo-Gothic style as had been the case with the castles of Rheinstein and Stolzenfels. A leading art historian named Paul Clemen, deplored the fact that too many battlements and arched mouldings had been added to the large rectangular structure with its corner turrets. Inside the tower there is a *beautiful collection of old Rhine views.* The castle is impressively situated, perched high on a crest of the hill over the "Soonecker Grund".

Owned by the Land Rhineland-Palatinate, Regional Office for the Protection of Ancient Monuments, Rhineland-Palatinate — Administration of State Castles. — Castle tavern, Museum. — Reached by car from Niederheimbach (Road B9); Car park. — 30 minutes walk from the Rhine Valley Road. — Open to the public with guided tours daily — except Mondays and except in December — from April to September from 9 a.m. to 1 p.m. and from 2 p.m. to 6 p.m. and from October to March from 9 a.m. to 1 p.m. and from 2 p.m. to 5 p.m. Last admission 30 minutes before closing time.

Hohneck Castle (also known as Heimburg) Picture on page 25

Above the long row of houses of Niederheimbach, the ivy-covered Hohneck Castle is lower down the hillside and thus closer to the river than

Sooneck Castle below Trechtingshausen · Text on page 48

any of the Rhine castles. The 13th century castle with its face wall towards the hillside and its 25 metre high keep, forms the northern defensive corner-post of the Mainz electorate against the electorate of the Palatinate. After being in ruins since the 17th century, it was rebuilt in the second half of the 19th century.

Owned by Paulheinz Kann. — Not open to the public.

Fürstenberg Castle Picture on page 29

The ruins of this castle situated on a rocky spur above the village of Rheindiebach, formerly served as a toll castle for the Palatine Electorate. The tower of the castle especially, attracted the attention of Victor Hugo who wrote of it as follows: "How strange is its extraordinary height and its unusual lay-out. It stands there with its high battlements but with no surrounding wall, no openings or windows and with hardly any arrow slits, its circumference and thickness increasing from the top downwards..."

In 1321 Ludwig of Bavaria besieged and conquered the castle which was first mentioned in 1243. Even he wished for nothing else here on the Rhine but to levy tolls from passing ships in order to fill his coffers. In 1632 Fürstenberg Castle was captured by the Swedes during the Thirty Years' War and in 1689, the fortress was destroyed by French troops and it has been in ruins ever since. Our photograph gives one a good idea of the old fortress and of the defensive value of the castle. Immediately behind the deep ditch on the side facing the hill, there used to be a gate-house, the former location of which is today just a heap of rubble. All that is left of its former so mighty surrounding wall is just an ivy-covered ruin. Of the palas or living quarters too, there is nothing to be seen but rubble overgrown with shrubbery. The tower alone which tapers to a height of 25 metres seems to have been built for eternity.

Owned by Vineyard Wasum, Bacharach. — Not open to the public.

Nollig Castle Picture on page 17

Situated on an elevation above Lorch at the end of the Wisper Valley, this castle once formed part of the town fortifications. First mentioned

Reichenberg Castle near St. Goarshausen · Text on page 59

around 1100. A tower furnished as a residence and two corner turrets on the side facing the hill have been rebuilt by the owner.

Owned by Fritz Wild. — Not open to the public.

Stahleck Castle

Pictures on pages 30, 33

The copper plate engraving by Wenzel Hollar shows Stahleck prior to its destruction by the Swedes in 1632. The artist sought to give an objective portrayal of the castle together with the defensive system of the town of Bacharach. One can clearly recognize the circular keep, two smaller towers and the stately palas or living quarters. The attacking front of the castle was that facing the hill. The side facing the Rhine seems invulnerable, protected as it is by the steeply sloping hillside and the town walls. The wall with its fortified turrets leading down into the valley — its remains are still clearly visible — unites town and castle in one powerful fortress.

Stahleck which is one of the most famous Rhine castles of the Middle Ages, was first mentioned in the year 1135. Originally it was the most southerly possession of the archbishops of Cologne; in 1190 the Emperor Barbarossa transferred ownership to his brother Konrad. When the latter's daughter Agnes secretly married her childhood friend Heinrich the Guelph, son of Heinrich the Lion, against the will of her father, the marriage taking place at Stahleck Castle, it brought to an end the bitter feud between the Staufers and the Guelphs. On the death of Agnes and of her only son who was childless, Emperor Friedrich II transferred the expired tenure to the Wittelsbacher Ludwig of Bavaria in 1214. Hence this powerful family then possessed with Stahleck and Pfalz Castles, two important bases on the Rhine.

The castle destroyed in 1689 was rebuilt as a superb reproduction of the original by the Rhenish Association for the Care of Ancient Monuments who placed it at the disposal of the German Youth Hostel Association for use as a castle hostel for young people. This association renovated the castle in 1966/67 on a large scale and completed the tower.

Owned by the Rhenish Association for the Protection of Landscape and Ancient Monuments. Hereditary building rights are held by the German Youth Hostel

The " Enemy Brothers" Sterrenberg and Liebenstein · Text on page 63

Association, Regional Organization Rhineland-Palatinate. — Reached by car from Bacharach. Car park above the castle. — 20 minutes walk from Bacharach. — Inspection only by appointment.

The Pfalz near Kaub

Pictures on pages 13, 14, 34, 58

"A ship of stone eternally floating on the Rhine, eternally at anchor in full view of the Count Palatine's town" (Victor Hugo), is the Pfalz formerly known as the Pfalzgrafenstein (Count Palatine's Rock) — one of the most curious fortified structures in the world. The only other castle to which it can be compared is, perhaps, Chillon Castle in Lake Geneva.

It was built as an island fortress prior to 1327, the year in which it is first mentioned, by King Ludwig the Bavarian for the purpose of levying tolls on the Rhine. From the spacious courtyard surrounded by pillared arcades and passages made of wood, the stumpy, pentagonal shaped tower rises. In the course of the centuries the shape of the roof of this tower has been changed on various occasions. The observation turrets protruding at the corners were constructed in their present form in the 17th century. The southern and northern ends of this "ship of stone" where there was also an entrance gate, were used as living quarters.

Owned by the Land Rhineland-Palatinate, Regional Office for the Protection of Ancient Monuments Rhineland-Palatinate. — Administration of State Castles. — Reached by ferry from Kaub. Inspection with guided tours from April to September from 9 a.m. to 1 p.m. and from 2 p.m. to 6 p.m. and from October to March from 9 a.m. to 1 p.m. and from 2 p.m. to 5 p.m. Last admissions 30 minutes before closing time. Closed on Mondays and in December.

Gutenfels Castle

Pictures on pages 14, 34

Built in the first half of the 13th century, this castle which was first mentioned in ancient documents in 1257, was in the possession of the Falkenstein family from which Archbishop Kuno von Falkenstein of Trier came. But only 20 years later the castle together with the town of Kaub lying at its feet, came into the possession of the Palatine Elector. It received the name Gutenfels in 1504 after the Landgrave Wilhelm of Hesse had beleaguered it in vain.

55

Liebenstein Castle above Kamp-Bornhofen · Text on page 63

The stately palas or living quarters has a large hall in each of its three storeys and the window arches of these halls are partly circular, partly pointed and in some cases even clover-leaf shape. The imposing 35 metre high tower is in a splendid state of preservation. "With its variety of late Romanesque shapes, Gutenfels Castle gives one an excellent idea of the structure and lay-out of a castle on the Rhine" (Paul Clemen). The fact that this is so is due to the Hessian archivist Habel, himself a castle lover, who acquired Gutenfels in 1833 intending to save this architectural monument. In 1886 the Cologne Cathedral architect Walther refurnished the castle.

Owned by Wilma Bartsch-Reichelt. Castle hotel. Notification necessary. Telephone: Kaub 06774-220. — Inspection not possible.

Schönburg Castle above Oberwesel

Pictures on pages 21. 57

The town of Oberwesel with its many spires and towers, extolled by Freiligrath as "the most beautiful refuge on the Rhine of the Romantic period", is dominated from the South by Schönburg Castle, the majestic grandeur of which makes it one of the mightiest castle fortifications on the Rhine. On the landward side is the "Hohe Mantel", the huge angular wall which is indeed an awe-inspiring structure designed to protect the two keeps and the living quarters. At a very early date the castle was recorded as an imperial tenure in the possession of the Lords of Schönenberg or Schomberg who provided the burgraves and overseers of Oberwesel. In the 14th century when it was the subject of dispute between the Reich, Trier and the Palatinate, it was enlarged by three branches of the family which also built their own castle houses known as "parcenary houses". The castle which, in 1689 together with the town, was gutted by fire and destroyed, was acquired in the 1880s by the German-American Rhinelander who, at very considerable expense, restored it. After the last war the part facing the Rhine was modernized but its ancient character was preserved and it was converted into an *International Kolping Youth Hostel.*

Owned by the town of Oberwesel. Castle hotel and restaurant. — Reached by car from Oberwesel station. Car park. — 15 minutes walk from the station along two winding paths leading off from Fahrstrasse. — Open to the public daily.

Schönburg Castle above Oberwesel · Text on page 56

Katz Castle

Picture on page 22

Prior to the year 1371 Count Wilhelm von Katzenelnbogen built the "Neu-Katzenelnbogen" Castle, popularly known as "Die Katz" (The Cat) on a narrow protruding rock overlooking the oldest part of the Loreley town of St. Goarshausen. Built as a fortified castle and military base, it was at the same time the castle extension to the residence and the connecting link between Rheinfels and Reichenberg. The structure is confined to the keep and the palas, both being linked by strong defensive walls. After having a storey added during the Hessian epoch, the circular keep with pinnacle reached the proud height of 60 metres. When in 1479 the male side of the Count's family died out, the castle passed to Hesse. During the French occupation Napoleon had this proud fortress demolished in the year 1806. During the 19th century the ruins changed ownership several times and it was not until 1896/98 that it was rebuilt on the basis of drawings by Dilich and in the course of the subsequent years several additions were made before it reached its present state. Today the castle is used by the Federal Social Welfare Organization as a holiday home and is the property of the German Federal Republic.

Owned by the German Federal Republic. Holiday home of the Federal Social Welfare Organization. Not open to the public.

Reichenberg Castle

Picture on page 50

Reichenberg Castle near St. Goarshausen, situated a few kilometres inland in the Hasenbachtal, is considered by art historians to be the most outstanding castle fortress in the Rhineland. The building was started by Count Wilhelm I. of Katzenelnbogen in the year 1320 to take the place of an older castle that had formerly stood there. But the plan was on such a grandiose scale that it was never completed. The wide protective wall extended between two slender circular towers. A notable feature of the castle is the three-storey hall building supported by pillars. As the floors have disappeared "three pillars stand one above the other, seeming to juggle with the high cross vault, a truly fantastic sight" (Richard Klapheck). Unfortunately the northern tower and parts of the wall collapsed in 1971.

Owned by Friedrich Holz. Inhabited. — Inspection impossible owing to danger of collapse.

59

The Pfalz near Kaub · Text on page 55

Rheinfels Castle

Picture on page 61

In the year 1245 Count Diether V. von Katzenelnbogen had the castle built for the protection of the St. Goar toll and within a short time it was developed into one of the most powerful castle fortresses in the central Rhine area. Only ten years after the commencement of the building work, *Rheinfels* Castle was successfully defended for a whole year in 1255 against a powerful army of the Rhenish League of Towns.

In the course of the following century the original toll castle became the increasingly important centre of administration of the Counts of Katzenelnbogen who, by their astute financial and marriage policy, became one of the leading families in the central Rhine area.

By the construction of the Neukatzenelnbogen Castle (today known briefly as *Katz* Castle) on the other side of the Rhine in the 14th century, the importance of Rheinfels Castle was further increased since the counts were now able to exercise complete and effective control of the Rhine valley.

When in 1479 the family of the Counts of Katzenelnbogen died out when at the height of their territorial power, *Rheinfels* Castle passed into the possession of the Landgraviate of Hesse. — Under the Hessian Landgraves *Rheinfels* was converted into a magnificent Renaissance castle and, together with its exterior fortifications, was enlarged to make it one of the most formidable fortresses in Germany. In 1692 *Rheinfels,* as the only fortress on the left bank of the Rhine, was successfully defended against the troops of Louis XIV. But when, in 1794, the fortress was surrendered without a fight to the French Revolutionary Army, the end of this proud castle had really come. In 1769/97 the castle together with its outer fortifications was demolished.

The visitor who inspects *Rheinfels* Castle today will be surprised at the vast extent of the ruins and at the maze of walled passages and underground adits which can still be walked along today. — But a really all-round impression of the military and cultural importance of the castle can only be obtained by studying the ancient plans and historical views of this once proud fortress, to be found in the former castle chapel where, today, the local history collection is housed.

Owned by the town of St. Goar. Partly inhabited. Local history museum. Restaurant and hotel. — Reached by car from St. Goar and from Hunsrück. — Car park.

The ruins of Rheinfels above St. Goar · Text on page 60

— 15 minutes walk from St. Goar. 45 minutes walk from Gründelbachtal (Hansen-weg). — Open daily during the summer season.

Maus Castle

Picture on page 62

Where there is a cat there must also be a mouse — that is what the Counts of Katzenelnbogen are reported to have said so scornfully of the new Trier electoral castle which, in the course of thirty years of building work from 1353 onwards had slowly taken shape above the town of Well-mich. The ulterior motive here, of course, was that the mouse would soon be caught by the cat and devoured. Its real name was originally Pe-terseck and then Thurnberg. The castle was ultimately completed by the great Trier Archbishop Kuno von Falkenstein who died here in 1388. Maus Castle is, architecturally, one of the most beautiful to be found along the Rhine. The almost square-shaped outline encloses a circular keep pro-truding from the main wall, a four-storey residential tower and the stately palas along the entire South side. Walled passages and the projecting corner turrets on all sides testify to the defensive nature of the castle and also to the fine intellectual spirit of that time. Between 1900 and 1906 the castle was carefully restored with laudable attention to historical detail.

Privately owned. — Not open to the public.

The " Enemy Brothers" Sterrenberg and Liebenstein

Pictures on pages 53, 54

The two castle ruins of Sterrenberg and Liebenstein which are situated on rocky crags above the ancient pilgrim town of Bornhofen are popularly known as the "enemy brothers".

Sterrenberg is the older of the two and as early as the 12th century it was in the possession of the Palatine family, the Lords of Bolanden as an imperial castle. Later it was owned by the Counts of Sponheim. Arch-bishop Balduin incorporated it in the Trier electorate. The square keep is still standing and the two protective walls can be clearly recognized. These walls were designed to screen Sterrenberg off on the side facing the hill and against the neighbouring castle.

Maus Castle above Wellmich · Text on page 63

Owned by the Land Rhineland-Palatinate, Regional Office for the Protection of Ancient Monuments Rhineland-Palatinate — Administration of State Castles. Inhabited. Castle restaurant. — Reached by car from Kamp-Bornhofen (B 42) via Burgenstrasse. Car park. — Footpaths from Kampen-Bornhofen: an easy walk of 30 minutes. By the steeper mountain path 15 minutes walk. — Open to inspection at all times.

Liebenstein Castle which was built at the end of the 13th century was a parcenary castle, passed later into the possession of Nassau-Saarbrücken and became a knights' castle (with Osterspay). The defensive keep seems to be growing out of the ground like a stump of rock. The seven-storey residential tower is partially preserved.

Owned by Dr. Freiherr von Preuschen, Osterspay/Rhineland. — Inhabited. Restaurant. — Rooms to let. — Reached by car from Kamp-Bornhofen (B 42) via Burgenstraße. Car park. — Footpaths from Kampen-Bornhofen: easy 30 minutes walk. Taking the rather steep mountain path via Sterrenberg Castle, 20 minutes walk. — Castle ruins open to the public at all times.

The Castle in Boppard

The Elector Balduin of Trier constructed one of the most formidable fortified buildings in the central Rhine area. The castle was built on the banks of the Rhine in order to consolidate the archiepiscopal rule that had been forced on the people of Boppard following the rebellion of 1327. At the end of 1499 the castle was destroyed by a big fire. But only a year later it was already rebuilt. However, the keep escaped damage in the fire. This is proved by the frescoes dating from the 2nd half of the 14th century to be seen on the top floor which made Balduin's castle an important place of interest. The castle houses the municipal local history museum.

Owned by town of Boppard. Local history museum. Pre- and early history, Thonet Museum. — Reached by car from the A 61, B 9 or B 42. Car park. — Open to the public from May to the end of September.

The Marksburg (Marksburg Castle)
Pictures on pages 9. 65

This castle towering on a high crag above Braubach, is the only fully preserved medieval fortress on the Rhine. At the beginning of the 13th century it was first known as "Brubach Castle" and belonged to the Lords

64

Marksburg Castle above Braubach · Text on page 64

of Eppstein. In the 13th century it passed into the possession of the Counts of Katzenelnbogen who turned it into a fortress. From 1479 to 1803 the Marksburg as it was known from the 15th century onwards, was under the uninterrupted rule of the Landgraves of Hesse and, thereafter, until 1866 of the Duchy of Nassau. In 1866 the castle together with the town of Braubach passed to Prussia and in 1900 it was purchased (at a price of 1000 Marks) by the *"Association for the Preservation of German Castles"* which had been founded in 1899. This association commissioned Bodo Ebhardt with the task of restoring it on the basis of structural drawings by Wilhelm Dilich (about 1607) and of fitting it out as a typical fortress of the late Middle Ages.

Located round a triangular courtyard are three asymmetrical wings of the building. The South side from which enemy attacks were to be expected, is protected by the "Kaiser Heinrich Tower" like a massive coat of armour. Behind a no less mighty wall is the East wing with the magnificent palas or living quarters together with kitchen, women's apartments and the Knights' Hall on the upper floor. The ancient keep rises from the centre of the courtyard. It is 40 metres high and has a commanding view of the countryside and is naturally also visible from afar. The circular top of the tower which was 8 metres high, was destroyed by the artillery of the 20th century in March 1945. It had previously been restored on the basis of Dilich's plans in 1906. But thanks to considerable state grants after the war, it was possible to repair the severe damage including that suffered by the keep itself so that the castle as a whole could be preserved. An irreplaceable cultural monument, "a superb example of medieval fortified and domestic architecture" (Magnus Backes) is today one of the most notable places of interest in the central Rhine region.

Owned by: Deutsche Burgenvereinigung e. V. Burgenforschungsinstitut. — Museum. Library of the above-named organization. Archives. — Reached by car from Braubach; car park. — 15 minutes walk from the town centre via Sommergasse; along the Rhine via Weinbergspfad, Martinskapelle — 40 minutes walk. — This castle — the only undestroyed hilltop castle on the central Rhine — is open to visitors at all times. Enquire at Castle Administration.

The Martinsburg in Oberlahnstein

Picture on page 80

The Martinsburg with its hexagonal keep was built on the banks of the Rhine at Oberlahnstein at the end of the 14th century and was used

The Queen's room in Stolzenfels Castle · Text on page 68

by the Electors of Mainz for the levying of tolls. Like the Trier bishops' castle in Boppard and that of the Cologne bishops in Andernach it was originally protected against the town by ramparts and ditches. The buildings are arranged round a square courtyard and display the architectural styles prevailing from the 14th to the 18th centuries. The palas or living quarters was built in 1500 and in 1712 the Gothic building was converted to the Baroque style. Today the Martinsburg houses the offices of local authorities as well as private apartments.

Owned by the Land Rhineland-Palatinate. Used partly by local authorities. — Reached by car from Oberlahnstein. — Not open to the public.

Lahneck Castle

Picture on page 79

Lahneck Castle is situated at the point where the River Lahn flows into the Rhine and is in a dominating position on the hill-top near Oberlahnstein. It was built in about the year 1240 as the most northerly fortress of the Mainz Electors. Around 1460 Dieter von Isenburg had the castle considerably strengthened by the construction of a new outlying protective wall. In the middle of the side exposed to attack to the south is the five-sided keep. On both sides of the keep a massive protective wall three and a half metres thick gives protection to the parts of the castle beyond, especially the palas or living quarters which forms the north wing facing away from the side most open to attack. By 1688 the castle had fallen into complete ruin but in 1860 it was restored to its original state.

Owned by Erbengemeinschaft Mischke Dr. Frhr. v. Preuschen. Inhabited, restaurant open throughout the year with garden terrace and café. — Reached by car from the B 42. Car park. — 5 minutes walk from bus stop. Along motorway 30 minutes. — Open to the public daily from Easter to October, courtyard, chapel, Knights' Hall, ascent of the tower. Open-air theatre August and September.

Stolzenfels Castle

Pictures on pages 66. 69. 70

Stolzenfels Castle is situated half-way up the hillside opposite the mouth of the River Lahn, a few kilometres above Koblenz. This former toll fortress belonging to the Electors of Trier, was started by Archbishop Arnold II. about the year 1250 and the electoral princes liked living there.

Stolzenfels Castle above Kapellen · Text on page 68
Pergola at Stolzenfels Castle · Text on page 68 · Picture on page 70

PLAN OF STOLZENFELS CASTLE

1 Entrance and castellan's residence, 2 Entrance gate, 3 Small banqueting Hall, 4 Large banqueting Hall,
5 Armoury, 6 Chapel, 7 Elisabeth's Tower, 8 Rough Tower, 9 Adjutant's Tower, 10 Arcades

But since the French invasion of 1689 it had been in ruins. The city of Koblenz made a gift of the ruins to Friedrich Wilhelm IV., later King of Prussia. Between 1825 and 1842 he had it rebuilt at considerable expense on the basis of plans by the most famous architect of his time, Karl Friedrich *Schinkel*. Although in restoring the castle the medieval sections were preserved, "a princely residence was created on the wooded heights in the neo-Gothic style and influenced somewhat by English castle architecture. However, it faithfully reflected the spirit of the age and of the royal master's wishes" (Paul Clemen). On the outside wall two murals by Lasinsky portray historical episodes. The furnishings of the living rooms date from the first half of the 19th century. In 1853 Ernst Deger adorned the Castle Chapel walls with paintings which are among the most mature works of the Düsseldorf Nazarene school. Today the castle is a *museum*. From the terrace one has a view of the village of Kapellen at the foot

73

The Archbishop's Castle in Andernach · Text on page 77 · Picture on page 71
The Fortress of Ehrenbreitstein · Text on page 74

of the mountain, overlooking the mouth of the River Lahn, Oberlahnstein and Niederlahnstein and downstream as far as Koblenz and Ehrenbreitstein.

Owned by the Land Rhineland-Palatinate, Regional Office for the Protection of Ancient Monuments Rhineland-Palatinate — Administration of State Castles. Museum — No direct access by road. Car park below the castle. — 10 minutes walk from the village of Kapellen. Inspection with guided tours from April to September on Mondays from 9 a.m. to 1 p.m. and from 2 p.m. to 6 p.m. And from October to March from 9 a.m. to 1 p.m. and from 2 p.m. to 5 p.m. except in December. Last admission 45 minutes before closing time.

Ehrenbreitstein

Picture on page 72

   The dominant hill facing Koblenz at the junction of the Rhine and the Moselle, is not only an outstanding feature of the landscape but was for centuries a point of the utmost strategic importance. Here the largest and most formidable Rhine fortress next to the Rheinfels at St. Goar, had been built. The Archbishops of Trier had the fortress constructed in the second half of the 12th century and at the end of the 14th century. In the years that followed practically every generation worked on it until ultimately it became the massive Renaissance fortress as depicted by Merian's engraving of 1646. In 1801 it was demolished by the French. But after the annexation of the Rhineland, it was rebuilt in the years 1815–32 by Prussia under the supervision of Colonel von Aster and became one of the biggest fortresses in Europe. And so it has remained although today it serves only peaceful purposes. Ehrenbreitstein houses: *the State Museum of History and Folklore (Land Museum of Technical Antiquities) and Rhine Museum* as well as a Youth Hostel.

Owned by Land Rhineland-Palatinate, Regional Office for the Protection of Ancient Monuments Rhineland-Palatinate — Administration of State Castles. 2 Restaurants. Youth Hostel. Film archives. Two museums (the Rhine Museum is the oldest river museum in the world). Fortress installations. — Reached by car from Ehrenbreitstein or via Niederberg. Car park by the fortress. — Chairlift. — 20 minutes walk from the B 42.

The German Corner

Picture on page 41

   The German Corner lies at the confluence of the rivers Rhine and Moselle. The Knights of the Teutonic Order gave it its name when, in 1216, they created a fief here. In 1945 the equestrian statue of Emperor Wilhelm I

The monastery Maria Laach at the Laacher See · Text on page 77

standing on the monument erected in 1897, was destroyed. With its inauguration on May 18th 1953 by Federal President Theodor Heuss, the monument became known as an "exhortation to German unity".

The Archbishop's Castle in Andernach

Picture on page 71

The castle in Andernach is the most magnificent of all Rhine town castles. Like the castle built in Boppard by the Elector Balduin, it was constructed by the Cologne Electors as a citadel, being protected against the town by a moat. In 1355 the townsfolk of Boppard stormed the castle and burnt it down. In 1496 it was enlarged by Archbishop Hermann IV of Hessen. In 1689 the French laid it in ruins again. All that remained were the rounded corner tower made of basalt lava from the Eifel Hills, three storeys high and above it the guard house with the protruding walled passage whence one has a fine view of the surrounding countryside; then there is the circular corner tower (powder tower) and the outer walls of the palas or living quarters.

Owned by Land Rhineland-Palatinate, Regional Office for the Protection of Ancient Monuments — Administration of State Castles. Youth Hostel. — Reached by car from Andernach. Car park at Stadtgraben. — Open to the public at all times as the ruins are situated in a public park.

Laacher See

Picture on page 75

The Laacher See lies in the heart of an ancient volcanic region. With its area of 331 hectares and its depth of 53 metres it is the largest of the crater lakes in the Eifel Hills. Its situation is particularly beautiful as it is surrounded by meadows and woods and belongs to a much visited National Trust area.

Maria Laach

Pictures on pages 75, 76

The Benedictine Abbey of "Abbatia Sancta Mariae ad Lacum" (Abbey of the Holy Mary on the Lake) was founded in 1093 by Count Palatine

77

The monastery Maria Laach · Text on page 77

Heinrich II. After difficult conversion work the church and convent were consecrated in 1157 by the Archbishop of Trier. It was not until the 19th century that the abbey was given the name "Maria Laach". In the Middle Ages the convent was renowned for its theological, artistic and cultural activities. After the French Revolution the convent was dissolved in 1802. But from 1863 onwards it was reopened and run by the Jesuits for ten years. In 1892 they handed it back to the Benedictines who again made it into a spiritual centre of international repute.

The Abbey Church with its six turrets is one of the most beautiful Romanesque churches in Germany. Due to its peaceful seclusion on the Laacher See the building which was designed as a "castle of God" is particularly well preserved and has retained its pristine beauty throughout the centuries. Among the features that are especially worth seeing are the masonry work in the atrium ("Paradise"), the frescoes on the pillars in the west chancel and the tomb of Count Palatine Heinrich. In the convent abbey there is a library containing 140,000 volumes.

Inspection all the year round. 30 minute guided tours at 10 a.m., 11 a.m., 1:30 p.m., 2:30 p.m. and 3:30 p.m. Parking facilities in the immediate vicinity.

Hammerstein Castle

The formidable rock with the ruins of this once so mighty castle dominate an extensive stretch of the Rhine valley. The castle was first mentioned as early as the year 1002 as the seat of the Hammerstein family. In 1020 it was conquered by Heinrich II. and made an imperial castle. Having been considerably enlarged by the Emperor Heinrich IV., it was used by him as a refuge when he was pursued by his son Heinrich V. and he brought with him the entire crown insignia. In 1374 it passed into the tenure of the Electors of Trier. It was only after the Thirty Years' War that this castle, which Merian's engraving portrays in its full medieval splendour, was razed and destroyed. Today all that remains of the vast structure are ruins apart from the massive keep and the outer wall which has the tremendous thickness of 5 metres.

Owned by the family of the Barons of Hammerstein.

Lahneck Castle above Oberlahnstein · Text on page 68

Rheineck Castle

Picture on page 83

This castle which was built by the Counts of the Palatinate on a wooded hill-top between Brohl and Bad Niederbreisig, was besieged and destroyed by the German King Konrad III. in 1151. In 1164 Rainald von Dassel, Archbishop of Cologne took possession of it. In 1282 Rheineck was destroyed for the second time. On this occasion Rudolf von Habsburg was responsible. Afterwards the Cologne Electors had the castle rebuilt and then in 1689 it shared the fate of most other Rhine castles. In 1832 an entirely new building was erected there by Joseph Carl von *Lassaulx*. All that remained of the original castle were the 20 metre high keep built of square blocks of stone and the Romanesque chapel. The paintings were done by Eduard von Steinle on behalf of the owner, Moritz August von Bethmann-Hollweg, for many years curator of Bonn University.

Owned by Natalie Hillebrand. Inhabited. — Not open to the public.

Arenfels Castle

Arenfels Castle on the outskirts of Bad Hönningen belongs to that category of Rhine castles that never experienced wars and which, in the course of the centuries were converted into peaceful hunting castles. This castle with its early Gothic keep was founded by the Counts of Isenburg around 1260. The two circular towers on the North front were added during the late Gothic period, whilst the 16th and 17th centuries brought the addition of the most beautiful Renaissance and Baroque parts. After the events of the Napoleonic era, Arenfels Castle under the Counts von der Leyen became almost a ruin. The purchase of the castle by the Counts of Westerholt saved it and it was rebuilt in the late neo-Gothic style by the Cologne Cathedral architect Zwirner. In World War II Arenfels was severely damaged.

Owned by Baroness von Geyr, partially inhabited. Restaurant at present closed. — Reached by car from Bad Hönningen, car park. — From Bad Hönningen, 15 minutes walk. — Not open to the public.

Landskron Castle

The Staufen fortress of Landskron is situated in the Ahr Valley near Bad Neuenahr on a cone-shaped hill and it dominates the surrounding

Martinsburg Castle in Oberlahnstein · Text on page 67

countryside. It was built by King Philipp of Swabia at the beginning of the 13th century not far from the point where the River Ahr flows into the Rhine. It was intended as a citadel against the Electors of Cologne and as a protection for the ancient Coronation Route from Aachen to Frankfurt. The ruins still testify to the former greatness of the castle which was destroyed in the 17th century, later passed into the possession of the Imperial Baron vom Stein and which today still belongs to his descendants.

Owned by Graf von Canitz, Cappenberg b. Lünen. — Reached by car via Lohrsdorf (bad road surface). Car park. — 45 minutes walk from Heimersheim, 30 minutes from Heppingen and 45 minutes from Lohrsdorf. — Open ruins on view at all times.

Dattenberg Castle

The castle which was a tenure of the Cologne Electors, was occupied by the Lords of Dadenberg, first mention of whom was in the 13th century. All that remains of the medieval castle are the Romanesque tower, the keep and the moat. The former palace has been converted into a youth training centre.

Owned by Erftkreis 5050 Hürth. — Reached by car along the B 42 or from Linz Station. — 20 minutes walk from Linz. — Not open to the public.

The Castle in Linz

The Cologne electoral castle situated on the Rhine front was built by Archbishop Engelbert in 1368. All that remains of it today is the tower crowned with a late Gothic superstructure in 1599. Everything else was changed in the Baroque period.

Owned by the town of Linz. Inhabited. — Reached by car. — Not open to the public.

Ockenfels Castle

Ockenfels Castle near Linz was the ancestral home of the zur Leyen family who had acquired it on tenure from the Cologne Electors. It was

Rheineck Castle · Text on page 81

destroyed in 1475. The Cologne architect Rheinhardt rebuilt it from the ruins.

Owned by Hermann May. Hotel, Restaurant. — Reached by car from Linz. Car park. — 30 minutes walk from Linz. — Open to the public at all times.

Roland's Arch Picture on page 84

The ivy-clad, legendary ashlar window that once solemnly looked down on to the Rhine island of Nonnenwerth, represents the last remains of Rolandseck Castle which was built in about the year 1100 by the Cologne Archbishop Friedrich. In 1334 it was refortified and then, in the fighting between the Cologne Electors and Emperor Friedrich III in the 15th century, it was destroyed. When the arch collapsed in the stormy night of New Year's Eve 1840, the poet Ferdinand Freiligrath, then living in Unkel, published an appeal in the "Kölnische Zeitung" for funds with which to rebuild the arch:

> "It is up to you! I stand here with begging hands,
> Up and down the Rhine I walk, admonishing as I go.
> Attendant of Roland, I hasten through the country;
> Open helmet in outstretched hand,
> I appeal to you: restore his arch to him."

The many donations received from castle-lovers all over the world enabled the arch to be rebuilt, the work being carried out by the Cologne Cathedral architect Ernst Zwirner. The owner of the Roland's Arch, Princess Marianne of Prussia, was at first angered by the autocratic action of the self-styled "Roland's attendant" Freiligrath. But ultimately she gave her consent and herself made a generous contribution to the cost of building a new elementary school in Rolandswerth.

Owned by Grand-Duke Ernst-Ludwig of Hesse and Rhine, Darmstadt. Restaurant. — Reached by car from Mehlem to Rodderberg. — From here 15 minutes walk. From Rolandseck and from Rolandswerth 30 minutes walk. — Open ruins always on view.

Drachenfels Castle picture on page 87

The wild, jagged Drachenfels towering so mightily above the river is not the only one of the Seven Mountains to have had a castle at its top.

85

Other peaks of the "Septimontium" or "septem montes" — first reported in the 16th century — were crowned with castles, such as the *Wolkenburg* and the *Löwenburg*. But only very scanty ruins of these castles are left. Visible far and wide, however, is the rugged keep of the Drachenfels built for the Cologne Electors, which is one of the rarer examples of a true ashlar structure. The view from the hill-top which is 321 metres high, is probably the most famous on the Rhine, just as the ruins themselves have rightly been described by Edmund Renard as "the proudest and most popular of the entire valley of the Rhine". On clear days the volcanic mountains of the Eifel can be seen, from the Laacher See to the "Hohe Acht". And to the north the spires of Cologne Cathedral can be seen.

This formidable mountain castle was started by the Cologne Archbishop Arnold I. (1138—1151). In 1149 it passed in tenure to the Bonn Cassius Foundation, whose dean, Gerhard von Are completed it by the year 1167. In 1176 the Cassius Foundation appointed the Knight Godart as the castle bailiff and his family adopted the name of the mountain and used the silver dragon facing to the right on a red background as its coat of arms. The legend of Siegfried is linked with this symbol for it was he who is said to have slain the dragon living in the mountain cave and to have bathed in its blood. Today the word "dragon's blood" has a more agreeable meaning, for it is the name given to the red wine produced from the vines growing on the southwest slopes of the mountain.

During the turmoil in and around Cologne the castle was occupied amongst others by 180 Bavarian riflemen who, together with Walloon soldiers successfully defended Königswinter on the 12th and 13th of September 1583. During the Thirty Years' War the castle was occupied in turn by the Swedes and the Spaniards to the pain and anguish of the people living in its vicinity. The Elector, therefore, ordered the castle to be demolished in 1634 and this was done with great thoroughness so that by 1642 one only spoke of the Drachenfels "ruins".

When work started on the building of Cologne Cathedral in the 13th century, the Drachenfels had to surrender its valuable trachyte stones. In fact the spot where the stone quarries lay is today still known locally as the "Cathedral hole". Finally continued irresponsible mining threatened to cause the remains of the castle to collapse. In 1780 the Castle Chapel collapsed. By degrees further parts of the castle collapsed also. And when even the top of the mountain itself was to be cut away, the Prussian

86

The ruins of Drachenfels Castle above Königswinter · Text on page 85